because
two are
better
than one

for you, Sister
Darlene

with love,
Liz

date
Mothers Day 2004

Our purpose at Howard Publishing is to:

- *Increase faith* in the hearts of growing Christians
- *Inspire holiness* in the lives of believers
- *Instill hope* in the hearts of struggling people everywhere

Because He's coming again!

You and Me, Sister © 2004 by Howard Publishing Co., Inc.
All rights reserved. Printed in Mexico
Published by Howard Publishing Co., Inc.
3117 North 7th Street, West Monroe, LA 71291-2227

04 05 06 07 08 09 10 11 12 13   10 9 8 7 6 5 4 3 2 1

Edited by Between the Lines
Interior design by LinDee Loveland and Stephanie D. Walker

ISBN: 1-58229-377-5

because two are better than one

you
and
me

Sister

HOWARD
PUBLISHING CO.

Printed in Mexico

Dee Appel and Jeanne Damoff

you

a

Your example of love, of living,
inspires me to reach farther.
To fly higher. To make
every moment count.

Sister

One's sister is a part of one's
essential self, an eternal presence
of one's heart and soul
and memory.

Susan Cahill

The Chewing-Gum Promise

Lynn's heart was racing almost as fast as her mind was. She felt a confusing jumble of emotions—exhilaration, fear, happiness, horror, guilt, hope, resolve, and self-satisfaction. She couldn't begin to unravel which was predominant, much less figure out what she should say to the gorgeous young man standing before her.

"So what'll it be?" he pressed. "Will you go out with me or not?"

"Oh, Mark," Lynn choked the words out. She could feel her cheeks grow hot and was dismayed to realize he could see her blushing. "It's complicated . . . " she started, then trailed off. "There are issues . . . " she tried again, but with no more success.

"Are you seeing someone else?" Mark asked softly.

Lynn shook her head no. She couldn't look at those eyes, so she focused on a chipped tile on the deck of the pool.

"Is it the way I look?" Mark kidded gently. "My prospects? My hygiene?" He cupped his hand to his mouth and exhaled, checking his breath.

Lynn laughed. "Oh, no, it's nothing like that," she assured him, finally daring to meet his gaze. She touched his arm and unexpectedly felt hard muscle. It flustered her again and brought the heat back to her cheeks.

For an agonizing moment, her resolve wavered. *Drat the old "chewing-gum promise,"* Lynn bemoaned inwardly. *How can I possibly explain this to Mark? How did I manage to turn a good thing into such a royal mess?*

The chewing-gum promise had seemed like such a good idea when she was ten. Lynn and her sister, Laurie, had been best friends for as long as either could remember. They did everything together. They acted alike, looked alike, dressed alike, and even talked alike. They called themselves twins, even though Laurie was thirteen months older than Lynn.

One day, when the sisters had grown pensive at thoughts of change and growing up, Laurie had proposed the chewing-gum promise. "Let's pick each other's husband. That way we'll be sure we can always stay close, like we are now. It would just be awful if we didn't like each other's husband!"

Lynn and Laurie had groaned at the thought. They each spat out their chewing gum and exchanged it to seal their pact.

They'd honored that pact on a few occasions during high school. Usually it was Lynn who vetoed a guy she knew was a loser, in spite of the charm he aimed at Laurie. Laurie, far more outgoing than her sister, had done her best to honor the chewing-gum promise by playing matchmaker for her quiet sister.

But last year in college, it was Lynn who thought she had scored a chewing-gum bull's-eye. When she spotted Kenny, she instantly believed he would be perfect for Laurie. Laurie had been unimpressed, but Lynn had seen past the greenish hair—an unfortunate accident involving a hair-care product and a chlorinated pool—to Kenny's heart of gold and quiet, steady nature. It took her awhile to realize that Kenny reminded Lynn of herself—so why wouldn't he and Laurie be perfect for each other?

Lynn had borrowed a few moves from her sister and played matchmaker. Soon it was apparent to everyone that Kenny and Laurie were perfect for each other. They set a wedding date.

But three months ago, Kenny had gotten cold feet and postponed the wedding. Hurt and upset, Laurie had cancelled everything and broken up with him. She had pined for Kenny ever since. That was the reason for this pool party. Today was the day Laurie and Kenny had planned to marry. Lynn had been desperate to find some way to distract her sister when she met the six young navy midshipmen visiting their church last week. Figuring the polite, good-looking young sailors would cheer her sister up and give her someone new to think about, Lynn had invited them to swim at the apartment the sisters shared.

When Laurie had joined Lynn inside to get more sandwiches and ice tea, Lynn had quizzed her sister hopefully. "Do you like any of them?"

Laurie looked out the window at the guys reclining on lounge chairs or horsing around in the water. "I like the one on the blue chair," Laurie announced. "Mark . . . he's the best one, definitely." She smiled thoughtfully. "I have a good feeling about Mark."

Mark it is, Lynn had told herself. She had focused her attention on Mark after that. She had to see if this guy was husband material for Laurie—and then work a little matchmaking magic.

That's how everything had gotten started—with the best intentions. Lynn's typical shyness and the awkward feeling she usually had around guys never showed up that day. She was relaxed and having fun as she focused on Mark and how compatible he'd be with Laurie.

She had liked Mark right away. Not only was he hot, but he was gentle and well-spoken. His eyes were kind, and his sense of humor had quickly captivated Lynn. This guy was perfect, she decided.

Too perfect. She'd pushed aside the momentary surges of connection and affection she felt for Mark. Laurie had specifically chosen this guy. What kind of a sister would try to steal him for herself?

Lynn had managed to keep her heart in check and her focus on her objective as she talked and laughed with Mark. Where had this come from? She had talked about Laurie nonstop, so she'd been totally unprepared when Mark asked her out. In spite of her horror at this development, she was also delighted and longed to say yes.

She looked over at Laurie, who was laughing and talking with two or three guys on the other side of the pool. For a fleeting second, the image renewed her hope. Laurie seemed to be having a great time with the others. Maybe she'd be happier with one of them, clearing the way for Lynn to be interested in Mark. Just this one time, when a really neat guy was interested in her, why was she letting her sister keep her from following her heart? Even as she dared to ask herself the question, she knew the answer. She loved her sister—more than she loved herself. She would do anything to keep from hurting her—to make her happy.

Just then, Laurie met Lynn's gaze, and their eyes locked meaningfully. A smile danced in Laurie's eyes. She paused and slowly blew a large pink bubble with her gum, then popped it deliberately. There was no mistaking the signal: Laurie was reminding her of the chewing-gum promise. With anguished guilt, Lynn grappled with a terrible thought: Her sister was screening guys for her, and she was repaying her by moving in on the one guy Laurie had expressed interest in since Kenny had broken her heart.

"So?" Mark asked again. "Why won't you go out with me? I thought we really connected."

"We have," Lynn agreed, chagrined. "But I think you'll really like my sister—"

"I'm sure I will," Mark responded, exasperated. "In fact," Mark said, grabbing Lynn's hand and drawing her after him, "maybe your sister will talk you into going out with me."

"No!" Lynn practically shouted. But Laurie, who had been heading toward the cooler, was already within earshot and arm's length.

"I sense you two need my help," Laurie laughed. "What can I do to help resolve this 'lovers' quarrel?"

Mark didn't bat an eye at Laurie's words, but they stopped Lynn dead in her tracks. Her heart seemed suspended in her throat.

"Mark, meet my sister, Laurie," she finally managed, weakly.

"I've heard a *lot* about you," Mark said. "Your sister thinks you're the smartest, best, most wonderful person in the world," Mark said, exaggerating each word as he said it. "So I thought maybe you could convince her to go out with me," he said lightly, but his eyes were earnest.

"I'd love to," Laurie said. She slipped between Mark and Lynn, put her arm around Lynn's shoulder, and steered her a few feet away from Mark.

"I . . . I can't . . . " Lynn sputtered. "You don't actually want me to go out with him, do you?"

"What's wrong," Laurie asked. "Don't you trust me to pick out a good one for you?" She smiled.

Lynn's mouth dropped open as the light began to dawn. "You mean when we were inside . . . You picked him . . . "

"I picked him for you," Laurie assured her. "I think he just could be the one."

Relief and excitement swept over Lynn. "But I was checking him out for *you*," she protested.

Laurie laughed. "Thanks, Sis, but that wouldn't make Kenny very happy."

"Kenny?" Lynn questioned, her eyes widening. "You mean . . . ?"

"Yes," Laurie said, her own eyes dancing with joy. "Kenny and I have been talking. We've worked some things out and are getting back together. We really do love each other, you know."

"I know!" Lynn agreed. "I guess I do know how to pick them for you after all."

Laurie nodded back to Mark. "And I know how to pick them for you." She spit out her gum and held it up. "After all, a promise is a promise—especially when you make it to your best friend in the whole world—your sister!"

Ten Weird Things
My Sister and I Like to Eat

1 *Cottage cheese on toast*

2 *Chili-dog pizza (sliced hot dogs, mustard, ketchup, relish, and chili)*

3 *Chocolate chip cookie dough—by the spoonfuls!*

4 *"Red Pixies" (sugar from Pixie sticks poured into the middle of red licorice)*

5 *Smoked oysters, sharp cheddar cheese, and salsa on Ritz crackers*

6   "Lizzards" (sautéed chicken livers and gizzards)

7   Cold pork-and-beans sandwiches

8   Raw pie dough

9   Butter slathered on both sides of white "balloon" bread and dragged through the sugar bowl

10   Spaghetti sandwiches (two pancakes with a slice of cheese in between, then covered with spaghetti sauce—heated, of course)

thank

you...

*for the countless times you've put
my needs ahead of your own.*

My Sister's Gift

You know how some people just have a special knack for finding you the perfect gift or saying the exact thing you need to hear at a certain moment? My dear sister has the corner on that market. In fact, she might have the whole block! I *try* to be thoughtful. She just *is*.

I finally figured it out. It took me a long time, but one day it dawned on me what was so special about her and how she pulls it off. She pays attention—to every detail and nuance. I might have mentioned something in a conversation or in passing that I had seen or drooled over and long since forgotten because it was a luxury I couldn't afford. Then, by some "sister magic," it would appear on the next special occasion, wrapped lovingly in a Victorian floral, because that's my favorite. More than once my sister has given me something dear to her own heart simply because I'd admired it.

It seems she never thinks of herself first. Instead, my sister pours out her generous love, and it spills all over me. She's always thinking of me and looking out for my best interests. It's an amazing feeling to be so loved. I hope someday I can learn to be as thoughtful as she is.

Thank you, my sweet, sweet sister, for all the times you've given me the gift of your close attention.

Make my joy complete by being

like-minded, having the same love,

being one in spirit and purpose. Do

nothing out of selfish ambition or

vain conceit, but in humility

consider others better than

yourselves. Each of you should

look not only to your own interests,

but also to the interests of others.

—Philippians 2:2–4

Dear selfless Sister,

One heart in two sisters—that's us. I love being on your wavelength! Your love completes me and brings me joy. I'm amazed and humbled by your regard for me. You're always looking out for my best interests, even at the expense of your own. I don't know what I did to deserve such a wonderful sister, but I'm glad you're mine!

Your devoted sister

You always know how to cheer
me up when I'm down.

A sister is a little bit
of childhood that
can never be lost.

Marion C. Garretty

The Gown Girls

"I think I'm going crazy." Abbey spoke into a cordless phone pressed against her ear by a cramped shoulder. Changing a diaper while trying to continue her conversation with her sister proved a challenge.

"You're not going crazy," Grace assured her. "You're just bored."

"I know I should love being a stay-at-home mom, but don't you ever miss putting on a power suit?"

Grace laughed. "Not really. My sweats are mi-i-i-ighty comfy."

"Humph. Laugh all you want, but I'm really starting to get depressed. And I know it's having an effect on Derrick and the kids. I'm not very nice to live with. Hang on a sec." Abbey sighed as she set down the phone and lifted Anna from the changing table. The baby smiled and cooed, but Abbey didn't respond. She placed Anna in the playpen, picked up the phone, and curled up on the couch. "OK, Grace. You've always been the one to cheer me up. What am I going to do? I don't think I can last much longer. I feel like I'm going to explode."

"Lots of moms would love to be able to stay home," Grace reminded her.

"Yeah," Abbey said, pushing a toy truck with the toe of her sock. "I'm grateful. But my days are filled with laundry, cooking, runny noses, and diapers. I hardly ever get to enjoy intelligent conversation with adults. When Derrick comes home, he's tired and doesn't want to do much. I joined that moms' group, but all we talk about is bathroom cleansers and potty training. Is this all life is?"

Abbey had been vice president of a successful marketing firm when she got pregnant with Stephen. She'd tried juggling a career and baby, but when she'd found out only ten months later that she was pregnant with Anna, she and Derrick decided she should stay home for a few years. Abbey loved the business world, but she also loved her family and believed the early childhood years were an important time of development. She just couldn't understand why it had to be so mind-numbing.

"Listen," Grace encouraged, "it's only three days until we all leave for Colorado. I have an idea. I'll tell you about it when we get to Mom and Dad's house. Right now I have to go. Sammy needs a bath, and it's time to start dinner."

Abbey hung up the phone. The thought of cramming luggage, six adults, and five kids into two vehicles for fourteen hours was hardly appealing. But Abbey looked forward to some good sister-time and couldn't stop wondering what scheme Grace was cooking up now.

Three days later, Abbey and her family met Grace's family at the sisters' childhood home. The whole tribe planned to rise early the next morning to set out for a week in the Rocky Mountains. Grace and Abbey knew it was up to them to prepare sandwiches and snacks for the road.

"We don't even get a break from household duties on vacation!" Abbey moaned.

"Oh? We'll see," Grace said with a wink.

The next morning the alarm clock jarred Abbey awake at 5 a.m. She sighed wearily and jabbed her husband in the ribs. "Welcome to Vacationville." Derrick groaned and pulled the covers over his head while Abbey dragged herself out of bed. When she switched on the light, she was surprised to see something hanging on the door. It was a formal evening gown. The red dress had spaghetti straps and a sequined belt. The skirt had calf-length, flowing, chiffon layers. The fitted bodice reminded her of 1940s or '50s evening wear she'd seen in movies.

What . . . ? Then a note pinned to the dress caught her eye. It was in her sister's handwriting: *Hey, Cordelia, Let's pretend! Love, Lady Lucille.*

Memories flooded in. Childhood games of dress-up. Abbey and

Grace ruling their kingdom as Princess Cordelia and Lady Lucille. Abbey laughed. *Does she want me to put this on now?*

"Cordelia?" Grace whispered through the door, "Are you dressed?"

Abbey opened the door. Grace stood before her, wearing a black evening gown with a matching neck scarf and cradling a loaf of bread in her arms like a dozen roses. "Time for the gown girls' royal sandwich making," she announced, grinning.

"And I thought *I* was going crazy! You, my dear, are gone!" Abbey shook her head but quickly added, "I'll be right out."

Abbey felt silly entering the kitchen in the red dress. *This is kind of fun, though,* she thought. Grace had already laid out the meat, cheese, condiments, and bread.

"Where did you get these dresses?" Abbey asked.

"I found them in the spare closet. They're Mom's old evening gowns," Grace announced delightedly. "You know she never throws anything away."

"Mary Poppins's advice wasn't wasted on you," Abbey said with a hint of sarcasm. "You'll make anything into a game!"

"Assembly-line sandwich making isn't the most stimulating task," Grace began in a mock British accent, "but what a difference a gown makes! Mustard spreads more easily; cheese slices fall into place with delicate grace." She exaggerated the words. "One can almost hear the symphonic accompaniment!" Grace stepped away from the counter and spun around, causing the layers of her skirt to swirl. She glided to the refrigerator and posed dramatically against the door.

"Gowns elevate the attitude and raise self-esteem," she continued, then suddenly stopped, frozen in midpose. "Wait! I've got an idea! We should start a business."

Abbey laid a slice of meat on a sandwich, glanced sideways at Grace and smirked. "What are you talking about? You're goofy."

"No, I'm serious. Don't you feel much better? Just think of all the women out there who need a motivational boost. They need to join us—the Sandwich-Making Gown Girls!"

Abbey and Grace laughed. Abbey had to admit that the sandwich detail had been a lot more fun than she'd anticipated. They changed into their travel clothes, hung the gowns back in the closet, dressed the kids, and got on the road by seven o'clock as planned. Between doling out snacks and toys and breaking up squabbles, the sisters managed to notice an interesting fact about highway construction crews: The workers who held the Slow signs were often women.

"I wonder if that woman likes her job," Grace mused as they passed yet another sunburned, sign-holding woman wearing a bright orange vest and hard hat.

"Looks boring," Abbey responded.

The sisters glanced at each other, and a sly grin tugged at the corner of Grace's mouth. Abbey understood.

"Gowns!" they exclaimed in unison.

"Those women should be given lovely gowns to wear while holding their signs," Grace said, her exaggerated tone returning.

"Yes," Abbey agreed, allowing herself to fall under the spell of the game. "It would improve their morale if they felt beautiful."

"They could be given tiaras and white gloves," Grace suggested.

"And they must be taught to wave properly . . . like Miss America," Abbey added, demonstrating the technique. "They could wave to all the motorists, brightening everyone's day!"

"We'll call our business Sandwich-Making, Sign-Holding Gown Girls," Grace announced. "Gown girls are multitalented. We mustn't limit them to sandwich making or sign holding alone."

They laughed at their own imaginations. After a while, though, the car grew quiet. The children napped, and Grace became engrossed in a book. Abbey stared out the window and thought about how much she missed lighthearted fun and laughter in her life. *Why am I so serious all the time? I wish I could be more like Grace.*

They arrived at the condo around 9:30 p.m. Grace and Abbey began unpacking.

"Grace," Abbey said, turning to her sister. "Do you always have fun?"

"Come on, Ab," Grace answered. "You know I don't. When Luke lost his job and couldn't find one for three months, that wasn't much fun. And when the twins caught the flu and Emma ended up in the hospital? Not exactly a party."

"Yeah," Abbey agreed, "but just in general you seem to enjoy life. You seem happy."

"I am, but not because everything's fun. I just try to make the best of every situation. Like when we were kids."

"But we're not kids anymore. Don't you wish you could break out of the motherhood prison now and then?"

Grace smiled. "Sure, I feel that way sometimes. But then I remind myself that my kids are growing up fast. They'll only be little for a short time. So as much as I can, I become Lady Lucille with them too. I try to remember what it's like to be carefree and happy."

Stephen toddled into the room wearing a saucepan on his head. "Gramma said I can play soldier," he lisped. "Mommy play too?"

"Mommy's busy," Abbey began.

"Eh, Cordelia?" Grace nudged her gently. "I think you'd make an excellent soldier."

"OK, honey . . ." Abbey relented, smiling. "Just let me get my helmet." She headed toward the kitchen, calling over her shoulder to Grace. "But where's a soldier without her gown?"

Grace laughed. "Spoken like a true gown girl! And a happy one."

Ten Things I Love
to Do with My Sister

1 Dressing up in outlandish costumes
and entertaining friends

2 Going into fancy
hotels or restaurants
and speaking
"French"

3 Singing songs
in harmony

4 Talking about
our families

5 Making up dance
moves to disco music

6 Going on trips with our families or girlfriends

7 Pretending to be serious about nonsensical ideas

8 Making her laugh hard—then laughing even harder with her

9 Discussing decorating ideas

10 Talking openly about concerns, fears, or problems, knowing the conversation will remain confidential

thank

you...

for listening—and for hearing
not only my words but my heart.

My Sister's Eyes

I love my sister's eyes. When she smiles or laughs, they crinkle into merry crescents, shutting almost completely. When we take an imaginary vacation into the land of make-believe, her eyes dance with fun. If I see a look of mischief there, I know I'm about to be drawn into some playful plot—pretending to be French in a public place or pulling a good-natured prank on a poor, unsuspecting soul.

My sister's eyes see the real me. She knows me, and she loves me anyway. I don't have to pretend to have it all together or say just the right thing. When I look into her eyes, I see acceptance. I see that she believes in me and admires me in spite of my sometimes selfish and inconsiderate ways. I see trust, and I want to honor it.

When I see pain in my sister's eyes, I pray its duration will be short. But I also understand that she will let the pain teach her—and afterward, her eyes will see with deeper sympathy and patience. When laughter returns, her eyes will dance with purer joy.

I'm blessed and thankful to have a sister who cares for me, inspires me, and brightens my days. Even when she doesn't say a word, my life is enriched by what I see in my sister's eyes.

I have indeed received much joy

and encouragement from your

love, because the hearts of the

saints have been refreshed

through you. . . .

—Philemon 7 NRSV

Dear wonderful Sister,

Don't we have fun? No one in the world is better at reaching the fun-loving little girl deep inside of me. With you, even the mundane tasks of life can be an adventure. Being with you—even thinking of you—always refreshes my weary heart. Thanks for your love and encouragement. Our friendship brings me great joy.

Your sister

My Sister

You are the only one of you,
There's none could take your place.
In everything you say and do,
You bring such style and grace.
You bless my heart because you are
Who God meant you to be,
And I'm so grateful every day
That He picked *you* for *me*.

—Dee Appel

Nothing makes me feel as special as a hug from you.

Sister

Having a sister is
like having a best friend
you can't get rid of.
You know whatever you do,
they'll still be there.

Amy Li

Priceless

Lisa and Janine possessed a treasure. For years it brought them great delight. Then they almost let it slip away.

As little girls, the two sisters built elaborate Barbie houses and played dress-up with their mom's clothes and jewelry. They snuck out of bed at night to play "let's pretend." As preteens, Lisa sometimes invited Janine to spend the night in her room. Janine would pack a bag as though she were going to a friend's house, and they'd stay awake talking, laughing, and listening to music. They tackled important topics too advanced for their youngest sister, Sherry—like which of the Monkees was cutest or what the hidden lyrics on the Beatles' album really meant.

When they were teenagers, the girls found different niches. Lisa hung with a longhaired, pot-smoking, guitar-playing, hippie crowd. Janine was a cheerleader who sang in the choir. Still, they enjoyed a friendship deeper than their diverse interests—a closeness developed through years of constant togetherness.

But everything changed the year Lisa went away to college. Janine still had three years of high school left, and during that time she and Sherry became more involved at church. In her sophomore year Janine had a deep religious experience that changed her life. Even with limited knowledge of her new faith, she knew she would never forsake it. And she couldn't wait to share her enthusiasm with Lisa when she came home for Thanksgiving.

Even before they got to the holiday table, however, Janine's hopes were dashed. "Oh, you have one of *those*," Lisa sneered when she saw Janine's ring with a Christian symbol—a little fish dangling from the silver band.

"I like it," Janine said defensively.

"I used to believe that stuff, but I've moved beyond that," Lisa said.

Janine couldn't mistake the derision behind her sister's comment. "I suppose you've found something better?" she challenged.

"As a matter of fact, I have," Lisa answered. "What I'm learning at the university has really challenged my thinking. The professors have encouraged me to open my mind and explore, both intellectually and spiritually. Christianity is rigid, narrow, and archaic. Universalism transcends your religion, Janine. It's a better way."

Janine saw no point in arguing. She didn't know the first thing about universalism, and she didn't know enough about Christianity to defend it to someone who'd been discussing theology with scholars. She couldn't change her sister's mind, but she wasn't going to let Lisa change hers either.

When Lisa returned home for Christmas break, she approached Janine with an air of authority and excitement, eager to share her own source of spiritual enlightenment. "This is such a great book! My eyes were really opened when I read it," she said, holding out a volume decorated with symbols that were foreign to Janine.

Janine wouldn't even take it from Lisa's hand. "I don't want to read that," she stated firmly.

"Why not?" Lisa snapped.

"I just don't." Janine was surprised at the fear and revulsion that rose up within her. She could barely understand it herself; how could she explain it to Lisa?

"Oh, come on," Lisa pressed. "It's just a book. It's changed my life. I want to share that with you. We can discuss what's in it."

"No!" Janine insisted, turning to leave the room. "I'm not going to read it. I don't want to know what's in it. Can't you understand that?"

From that time on, it was as though something had died between the two sisters. Janine felt uncomfortable around Lisa—a chill that even the magic of the holidays didn't thaw. She didn't like this feeling, and she tried to laugh and joke with her sister as usual. But her attempts fell flat. Lisa had withdrawn.

When the break was over, Lisa left early in the morning—not even bothering to wake Janine for their customary good-bye hug. Janine felt the sting. She was rebuffed and a little angry, but mostly sad and confused at the change in their relationship. They had always held different views, but they also had always allowed each other that freedom and remained close at heart. Small rifts were quickly mended. But this felt big, and Janine didn't know how to fix it. All she could do was hope—and pray—that Lisa would come to understand why Janine couldn't share her book or her faith.

In a few years, Janine went to her own college of choice. Holidays at home still seemed strained between her and Lisa. She chalked it up to the inevitable changes of growing up and growing apart.

After college, Janine married and started a family. Lisa pursued an acting career that took her to New York City. Janine followed the teachings of Jesus. Lisa embraced a New Age philosophy. They kept in touch but seldom discussed spiritual matters or anything that went deeper than the surface.

Each year at Christmas, the girls' parents invited everyone to come for an extended visit. One day, while Lisa and Janine sat talking in their old playroom—a scene of countless childhood delights—Lisa became pensive.

"What are you thinking about?" Janine prompted her sister. She was shocked when Lisa unleashed a torrent of angry words and pent-up emotions.

"Do you remember the time I tried to get you to read that book?" Lisa sneered, but her lower lip quivered.

Janine hesitated. What would bring this up more than ten years later? She answered cautiously, unsure what to expect. "Yes, I remember."

"That was important to me," Lisa spat the words accusingly. "And you wouldn't even look at it. You hurt me."

Janine was taken aback at the intensity of her sister's feelings. She wanted to defend herself but decided to listen instead.

Having opened the floodgate, Lisa's feelings spilled out in a torrent. "I wanted to talk to you about what was going on in my life. I was excited about what I was learning, and I really wanted to share it with you. But all you cared about was your own religion. You pushed me away." The anger that burned in her eyes softened, and she looked away. "And sometimes I think you've been pushing me away ever since. Things have never been the same between us."

Janine was speechless. She hadn't realized how threatened and left out Lisa had felt. Now she saw that the book had been Lisa's attempt to build a bridge to her sister. Janine bit her lip as understanding sunk in. When she had refused to read Lisa's book out of her own insecurity, her sister had taken it as a personal rejection. Her wound had festered all this time. Janine was humbled and alarmed to recognize how her insensitivity so many years ago had practically destroyed their precious relationship.

When she spoke, it was with quiet sincerity. "I'm sorry I hurt you, Lisa. My refusing to read the book was no reflection on my love for you." She paused, gathering her thoughts. "I just *couldn't* read it. I was afraid of it. My faith was too new—too fragile."

She paused and studied Lisa for signs of understanding. "If you want me to read it now, I'd be happy to."

Lisa's anger seemed to have spent itself. She sighed, then spoke softly: "No. I don't care about that anymore." She looked away.

Janine looked down at her hands. "I'm glad you talked to me about this. I had no idea the book mattered so much. Please forgive me for hurting you."

"I just wanted us to be close, and we were so far apart," Lisa said, vulnerable enough for the first time in years to let Janine see her tears. "When I came home from college, I could see you and Sherry had the same faith and were growing closer, and . . . well . . . I was jealous. It seemed like you didn't need me anymore—like Sherry had taken my place in your life and your heart." She wiped her tears and smiled a little. "When we were kids, you and I did everything together, and she was just the little sister."

"Oh, Lisa!" Janine put an arm around her sister's shoulders and touched her head to Lisa's. "Sherry could never take your place in my heart. I want us to be close too! It's OK that we aren't exactly the same. Let's face it," she said, giggling through her own tears, "we were pretty different as kids. It didn't stop us from being close then, and it doesn't have to now." She looked her sister in the eye. "I love you," she said firmly. "I always have, and I always will."

The two women embraced in a long, tight, healing hug. When they parted, Janine caught her breath at the wide, unguarded smile on her sister's face. "Wow," she said with a reciprocal grin. "I haven't seen that in about ten years—I've missed it." Janine relished the moment. That smile, like her relationship with her sister, was priceless.

Ten Dream Goals
My Sister and I Share

1 *Singing with a live jazz band*

2 *Snow skiing in the Swiss Alps*

3 *Riding in a gondola in Venice in the rain*

5 *Dancing with our favorite movie star*

4 *Sipping lattés at a Paris café*

6 *Living in a foreign country for a year*

7 *Going on an African safari*

8 *Learning to surf in Hawaii*

9 *Going skydiving*

10 *Writing a book about all our adventures*

thank

you...

for loving me no matter what.

My Sister's Acceptance

Life is filled with opportunities for rejection. Employers, coworkers, even trusted friends have at times wounded my heart with cruel or thoughtless words and actions. But I have someone in my life who always accepts me as I am—my sister.

My sister knows me better than anyone else does, because she has been with me through every stage of my life. She understands who I am and what made me this way. And she loves me in spite of all my imperfections.

If I need some time just to be quiet, my sister isn't offended. We can ride for hours in the car in silence without a single awkward moment. The acceptance between us is felt even when unspoken.

Growing up, we had to learn to share, to communicate, and to forgive. A history of whispered secrets and late-night laugh sessions provided a foundation for a lifetime of friendship. True friendship. Reliable friendship. If the whole world turns against me, I know where I can go. The acceptance my sister offers reminds me that I am valuable and precious—and that she is.

If someone can know me as well as she does and still love me as much as she does, I know I can handle any other rejection that may come my way. Whatever happens, I know I'll always find love and acceptance with my sister.

Above all, love each other deeply,

because love covers over a

multitude of sins.

—1 Peter 4:8

Dear long-suffering Sister,

I've always loved and admired the gifts, abilities, and ideas you've had that were different from mine. What I value most is the way our deep love for each other has forever melded us together, in spite of our differences, sisterly disagreements, and diverse ways of seeing things. You've covered a multitude of my mistakes and insensitivities with the depths of your awesome love for me.

Your loving sister

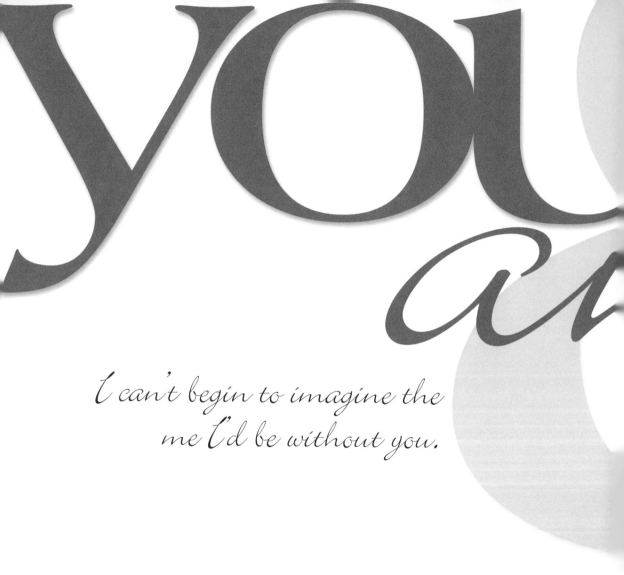

I can't begin to imagine the me I'd be without you.

Sister

A sister is one
who reaches for your hand
and touches your heart.

Author unknown

Through the Dog Days

August brought yet another sticky-hot daybreak. Denise lay staring at the ceiling of her Victorian bedroom, listening to the silence that exaggerated the emptiness she already felt.

Silence could be really loud, she decided.

The children were grown, the last one moved out. Her many years of single parenting blurred in her memory like a fast-passing freight train.

There was only one break in the quiet. Curled behind her knees was her faithful companion of thirteen years, snuffling softly. Once she'd had a "real" name, Denise recalled, but somehow the little Yorkie had laughingly become known as Widgie. All four pounds of her.

Widgie had come at another time when Denise needed comfort. She was so tiny; Denise carried her around zipped inside her winter jacket, and half the time no one even knew she was there. She had been smuggled into movie theaters and restaurants, even into Denise's office in an upscale city building, and her sweet temperament and excellent traveling skills had won many hearts.

Denise's sister, Julie, had bought Widgie as a surprise for her fortieth birthday. As it turned out, that was also the year Damien, Denise's husband, had another less pleasant surprise in store for her. He had decided he needed more excitement in his life and left Denise with three small children—and Widgie. Julie never said a harsh word about Damien. She just brought in dinners, bathed the children and read them to sleep, and held Denise's hand through the paralyzing time of realizing she was truly on her own. Julie had stood guard on one side of Denise's heart, and Widgie had warmed the other.

Denise sat up and began extricating herself from the sheets, working at not disturbing Widgie. Denise hadn't told Julie yet that Widgie was failing. Mostly because she couldn't quite admit it to herself. But the accidents on the carpet were happening all the time now, and sometimes the little dog was vomiting spots of blood. Widgie often greeted Denise at the door with her head hung, as though she were ashamed of herself. It was completely out of character for her, and multiple trips to the veterinarian had not resolved the problems.

Widgie had come to represent the last vestige of "family life." And now the inevitable loss was on the horizon. Denise swallowed hard, forcing back the tears, as she dressed for her Saturday outing with Julie.

For the past thirteen years, on the first Saturday of each month, Denise had met Julie for tea, and both sisters loved the ritual. They had discovered some of the most incredible, charming, and welcoming places within just a hundred miles. Regardless of the gloom of any given day, Denise was always soothed by Julie's warmth, comfort, laughter, and understanding.

On this Saturday, as Denise followed the map to meet her sister, she began to wonder whether she would *ever* reach the teahouse. The route appeared simple enough, but the drive seemed endless. At last she rounded a corner on the delightful country lane and caught her breath as she took in the spectacular Victorian home. She parked and entered the surrounding classic English gardens, then spotted Julie waiting for her among sapphire hollyhocks.

"Hey, Sis, I was beginning to wonder if you'd gotten lost," Julie said with a welcoming smile. She linked her arm through Denise's, and together they walked through the front archway that dripped with wisteria in full bloom. Denise inhaled deeply and sighed.

A hostess led the sisters to a table tucked next to a bay window. The gardens were in full summer regalia, flooding Denise's soul with a much-needed respite. Just after high tea was served, Julie reached down by her purse and retrieved a lovely gift bag. It looked like a Victorian teahouse. Pretty fuchsia tissue paper arranged in festive peaks rose past the top of the bag. "This is for you," Julie said, handing the package carefully over the teapot to her sister.

"It's not my birthday," Denise said with curiosity. "What's the occasion?" Even as she asked the question, she plunged her hand into the bag and wrapped her fingers around something soft and plush. She pulled from the hot pink cloud of tissue what could have been Widgie's twin, right down to the fuchsia bow between her perky ears. Denise halfway expected the toy to give her a "wet-Widgie" kiss.

"For someday," was all Julie said.

Tears stung Denise's eyes as she realized Julie was well aware of her beloved pet's waning health and how hard the letting go would be. "Thanks, Sis," was all she could manage.

Unbidden, the waitress arrived with a fresh pot of tea and strawberry scones, providing a break in the emotional intensity.

The topic of conversation turned to Denise's children. Auntie Julie loved to hear every single detail of their lives. Julie believed "unbirthdays" were even more fun than the real thing, and she had lavished extra love on them over the years they were absent a father. They all adored her, and Julie's devotion to them had always been a huge source of comfort to Denise. Sometimes during those long single-parenting years, Denise was quite sure she would have lost her sanity if not for Julie's stable and unflappable influence.

"Well, Jules, I need to get back to the house and check on Widgie."

"I should get home and finish up in the garden," Julie responded. They paid the bill, stood, and moved toward the floral archway, leisurely passing through the heady blended scent of honeysuckle and roses.

When they reached Julie's car, Denise gave her sister a warm hug and whispered her thanks again. She felt doubly warmed—by the day and by the blessing of her sister's love. *She understands me from the inside out and knows my need without my even having to ask,* she thought. *Kind of like God. Yes, a lot like God.*

Denise pulled into her driveway at home, ran up the few steps to her door, and put her key in the lock. Widgie met her as she entered the house—tail wagging, but head hung low. A stab of impending grief struck Denise's heart. She bent over and picked up her loyal companion, snuggling her into her neck. "It's all right, old friend. It's not your fault. I know you can't help it."

A few minutes later, Denise put the beautiful bag from Julie down on her bed and pulled out the little stuffed Yorkie. She noticed for the first time a tiny tag attached by a delicate silk ribbon around its neck. Denise flipped open the tag and read Julie's lovely handwriting: *When the time comes, let me take her for you. I love you, always. J.*

The tears came then. Tears of release. Tears of loss and change. Denise gave in to the flood of raw emotion. When her weeping subsided, she blew her nose and set the gift on her chenille bedspread.

As if events had lined up to prepare her, it was only a few days later that Denise knew the time she dreaded had arrived. She awoke to several spots where Widgie had been sick during the night, and her pet was very lethargic. She could barely bring herself to think of calling Julie . . . when the phone rang. After only hearing her sister's

"Hello," Julie seemed to know what was happening. "I'm on my way," she promised.

The rest of the morning was a blur, with Julie arriving to fold her sister in her arms. "It's the right thing to do," she reassured Denise. "You don't want her to suffer." Denise nodded in wordless agreement. Julie scooped Widgie into a small towel and went out the door.

Denise's heart constricted with loss, knowing she had said her final good-bye to her tiny companion, and she wept deeply.

Less than a half-hour later, Denise heard cars in the driveway. First her sons arrived together, followed by her daughter. She realized they must have responded to a request from their aunt and dropped everything to come to her. One by one they hugged her with the understanding that comes with adulthood. The four of them sat together in the living room as a family. They laughed and cried as they shared sweet memories.

When Julie's car pulled back into the driveway, Denise stayed behind as her children went to greet her. She watched from the bay window as the boys dug a small grave under the willow tree and her daughter and sister stood by. Her big, strapping sons transplanted a giant sunflower to mark the spot and wrote "Widgie, 1981–1994" on a huge rock—an acknowledgment of the big role in their family played by this tiny creature. From her vantage point, Denise could make out tears on their cheeks too, a reminder of the little boys still inside them.

Julie looked up to the window, and her eyes met Denise's. An expression of compassion and understanding shone from Julie's face. Denise understood that her sister was being the hands and heart of God, caring about the smallest details of her world, just as He does.

Denise turned her back to the window, and her eyes fell on the miniature plush toy standing watch on her bed. She knew it would always be a reminder of thirteen joyful years of companionship—and the lifelong blessing of a sister's love.

Ten Therapies My Sister and I Share

1 *Lying on our backs and counting falling stars during a meteor shower*

2 *Riding the Ferris wheel or carousel at a summer fair*

3 *Speculating about our dream vacations*

4 *Taking an impromptu drive to the beach for breakfast or lunch*

5 *Eating cotton candy and pretending we're not too old to*

6 *Running barefoot through a summer rain*

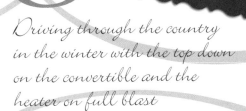

7 *Singing old camp songs around a driftwood fire on the beach*

8 *Driving through the country in the winter with the top down on the convertible and the heater on full blast*

9 *Giving each other pedicures and painting our toenails bright, fun colors*

10 *Relaxing head-to-toes in a double hammock, swinging and laughing about how lazy we are today*

thank

you...

for the warm light of your presence—and
for letting me bask in your glow!

My Sister's Heart

I've always thought of it as a mercy heart. My sister is one of those special people who's right there with you, no matter what. She always seems to sense what I'm thinking or feeling. It's as though she were inside my own skin, sharing my soul.

Looking back, I can't remember a time that she wasn't the first one I thought to run to—when I got in trouble for taking the car without permission and Dad grounded me for a whole month! When a boy I thought had never even noticed me asked me to the prom. When that boy eventually asked me to marry him!

She held my bouquet and wept tears of joy for me the day I was wed; and when I miscarried my first child, she cried with me as if it were her own loss. Two years later, she was there to photograph and celebrate the birth of my beautiful daughter. The tears we shared that day seemed to come from a place I didn't even know existed, a well that must have been filled by the angels in heaven.

My sister is the epitome of unconditional love. She anticipates my needs and loves me sacrificially. I can trust her to always speak truth to me. And I can count on her to share the ups and downs of life, to walk with me through whatever comes. That's my sister—my friend.

I will be glad and rejoice in your

love, for you saw my affliction and

knew the anguish of my soul.

—Psalm 31:7

My precious Sister,

How can I ever thank you for your love? I've always felt it—always known you were there for me. But never has your love been so refreshing, so sustaining, as when troubles and sorrows darkened my skies. Friends, hope, and happiness seemed swallowed up in the darkness. But you knew my anguish and my need for you. You were there, supporting me, loving me, and walking with me.

Your grateful sister

Kind heavenly Father,

Thank You for this sister You've given me. She's the best! It seems You knew exactly what I needed to challenge me, delight me, halve my sorrows, and double my joys.

Thank You for giving me a glimpse of Your changeless, extravagant love through my sister. Like You, she's always rooting for me, glad for my successes, indignant when injustice touches my life, and proud of me. No wonder I stand a little taller, hold my head higher, and smile a little broader whenever I'm with her. I can turn to her with exciting news, scary problems, or when I just need to talk things out.

Please bless her. Reward her for her patience, kindness, and friendship. Help me to be for her the kind of sister she has always been to me.

Amen